My Mother Always Used to Say

Mysterious wisdom
many a mickle makes a muckle

A wise precaution
take a cardigan

On learning by example
don't do as I do – do as I say

Heartbreak
you're better off without him

Anna Tochter

My Mother Always Used to Say

HarperCollins*Publishers*

HarperCollins_Publishers_

My Mother Always Used to Say... first published in 1993
My Mother Always Used to Say That Too... first published in 1999
This edition, comprising material from both books, first published in 2004
by HarperCollins_Publishers_ Pty Limited
ABN 36 009 913 517
A member of the HarperCollins_Publishers_ (Australia) Pty Limited Group
www.harpercollins.com.au

Compilation copyright © Anna Tochter 1993, 1999, 2004
Illustrations copyright © Fontaine Anderson 2004

HarperCollins_Publishers_
25 Ryde Road, Pymble, Sydney, NSW 2073, Australia
31 View Road, Glenfield, Auckland 10, New Zealand

Tochter, Anna
    My mother always used to say.
    ISBN 0 7322 8015 X.
    1. Mothers – Quotations, maxims, etc. I. Tochter, Anna My
    mother always used to say that too. II. Title.
082.0852

Cover and internal design by Gayna Murphy, HarperCollins Design Studio
Illustrated by Fontaine Anderson
Typeset in 13/18 Gill Sans Light
Printed in Hong Kong by Phoenix Offset on 140gsm Woodfree

Happy mothersday mama
love Siena and Iain xoxo

2004

To my mother who always used to say …

'You'll understand when you have children of your own.'

And now I do.

Introduction

Like many women, it took having children of my own (and a daughter especially) to make me fully appreciate my own mother and the debt I owed her. Time and time again, my mother's words come back to me as I hear myself saying, 'My mother always used to say …' Generations of accumulated wisdom pass down the female line this way, from mother to daughter. I have no doubt that one day my daughter will carry on the tradition.

We are all the product of our mothers and their mothers before them. A funny mixture of values and prejudice, old-wives' tales and good old commonsense leaves its mark on the adult. To this day I cannot have my ears pierced or eat in the street.

Mothers were our guide in all things and knew everything, they were our first inspiration, they loved us and wanted us to grow up a credit to them. They set the rules and when reason failed they had the last, irrefutable word —

because I am your mother and I say so!

Anna Tochter

On bringing up children

You give your children two things:
you give them roots and you
give them wings.

Nice girls don't …

Mothers always assume that they are bringing up a nice girl and that other girls are bad influences. Nice girls were always identified by a series of things they didn't do …

Get their ears pierced.

Wear black underwear.

Eat in the street.

Smoke in public.

Swear or make a fool of themselves with drink.

Dye their hair.

Wear jewellery that makes a noise.

Wear shoes that need heeling.

Make the first move.

Get in the front of taxis.

Check out the labels on presents.

Bad girls

Men don't marry girls like that.

Other people

Otherwise known as 'But everyone else does it' …

I don't care what *other* mothers do!

Just because everyone else is doing it, doesn't make it right.

If everyone else was jumping off a cliff, would you do it too?

Beauty care

From the first attempts at make-up and wanting to lock the bathroom door, mothers were (unfortunately) always there with helpful advice …

You don't need make-up at your age.

Never pluck your eyebrows.

You make your own face.

If you pluck out one grey hair another seven will grow in its place.

Brush your hair one hundred times before bed.

If you start shaving your legs now, you'll have to deal with the bristles for the rest of your life.

One hour's sleep before midnight is worth two after.

If you don't keep your face out of the sun, your skin will look like leather by the time you're 25.

Precautions I

Always wear clean underwear in case you're run over by a car and have to go to hospital.

Hygiene

Not to worry, we all have to eat a bit of dirt before
we die.

Don't put that in your mouth, you don't know where
it's been.

There's no substitute for clean fingernails.

Is that a real wash, or just a lick and a promise?

Acne and other agonies

It's just a phase.

Don't squeeze it.

Don't scratch it.

If you pick it, it'll never get better.

If you pick it, it'll leave a scar.

The lovely April
of her prime …

Thou art thy mother's glass, and she in thee
Calls back the lovely April of her prime.

William Shakespeare, *Sonnets 3*

I know you find it hard to imagine, but I was once
considered good-looking.

Childbirth ruined my figure.

Maternal bias

You can't improve on a miracle.

Beauty is in the eye of the beholder.

Anyway, you have a lovely personality.

Looks aren't everything.

Beauty comes from within.

It's just puppy fat.

You'll grow out of it.

No boy wants to date a broom handle.

Keeping up appearances

It doesn't matter about your clothes provided you have good-quality shoes.

Ill-fitting shoes show on your face.

Lift up your feet when you walk, you don't want to wear out the ground.

Clothes

You only need three of anything:
one on, one in the wash
and one in the drawer.

Mother knows best

Mothers had an (often contradictory) saying for everything and all occasions …

Better out than in.

Empty vessels make the most noise.

If you can't be good, be careful.

Don't care was made to care.

Out of sight, out of mind.

Don't make a fuss.

The devil makes work for idle hands.

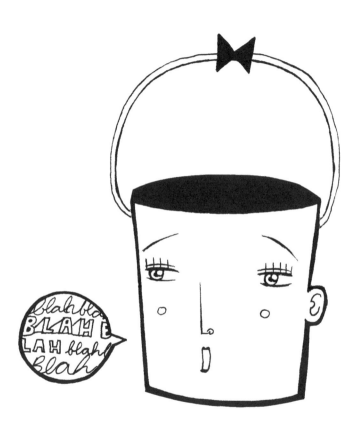

Hear no evil, see no evil, speak no evil.

Neither a borrower nor a lender be.

Monkey see, monkey do.

Better safe than sorry.

There will be tears before bedtime.

Don't make mountains out of molehills.

She's no better than she should be.

If you don't stop that you won't be able to help it.

More haste, less speed.

If a job's worth doing, it's worth doing well.

A thing learned now is a habit for life.

Funny ha ha or funny peculiar?

It's never too soon to learn.

Were you behind the barn door when brains were being given out?

Were you born in a tent?

All things in moderation.

If you go to bed with wet hair, you'll catch your death of cold.

Please and thank you

I didn't hear the magic word …

Manners maketh daughters …

Oh, the hours of work that went in here …

When someone asks you how you are, don't tell them!
Say: 'Very well, thank you'.

Protect yourself from other people's bad manners
by a conspicuous display of your own good ones.

Manners are all we have to separate us from the animals.

Do unto others as you would have them do unto you.

Thank you letters must be written within the month.

Don't make personal remarks.

Don't point.

Don't whisper.

Children should be seen and not heard.

Speak when you are spoken to
and not before.

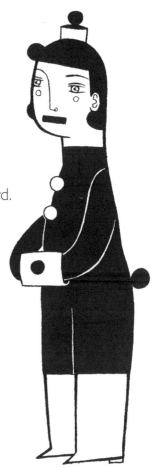

Table manners

In between the admonishments we managed to get something to eat …

Elbows off the table, hands in laps.

Don't speak with your mouth full.

Don't read at the table.

Flags were made for waving, not forks.

Don't start until your mother is served.

A lady never eats everything on her plate, she leaves something for Miss Manners.

Food

Crusts will make your hair curly.

Carrots will make you see in the dark.

Eat your greens or you'll get warts.

Eat your spinach and you'll get strong.

Chew it properly.

Don't play with your food.

How do you know you don't like it if you
haven't tried it?

Waste not, want not.

Eat that up! Don't you know there are starving
children in India who would love that?

There'll be no pudding till you've eaten everything on your plate.

The art of delegation

It's no good keeping a dog and barking yourself.

Mysterious wisdom

Many a mickle makes a muckle.

Maternal martyrdom

(sometimes known as the Burnt-chop Syndrome)

No, it's fine, I've eaten.

You have the last piece.

Of course I don't mind.

Night-time

Never disturb a sleeping child.

There never was a child so lovely but her mother was glad to see her asleep.

Why aren't you in bed?

Eating late at night will give you nightmares.

Only children with a bad conscience can't sleep.

If I have to come upstairs once more, there will be serious trouble.

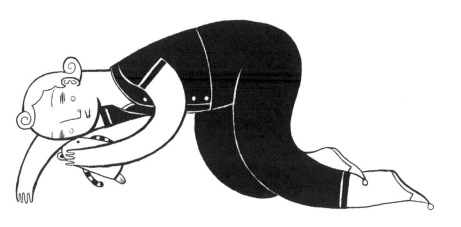

very, very good

horrid

Can this be me?

There was a little girl
who had a little curl
right in the middle of her forehead;
when she was good she was very, very good,
and when she was bad she was horrid.

Henry Wadsworth Longfellow

Punishment

I'm only doing this for your
own good.

You'll thank me later.

This is going to hurt me more than
it's going to hurt you.

Precautions 2

Always put paper on a
strange toilet seat.

Why?

… because it's good for you.

… because I say so.

Don't say …

couch

ta

toilet

beg yours

pardon

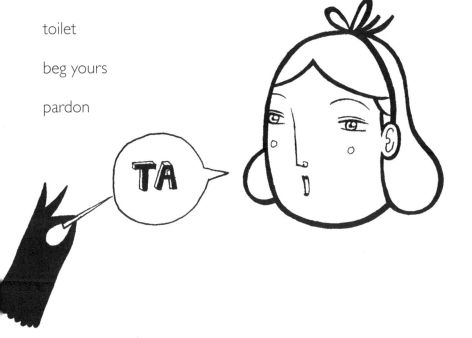

Naughty little girl

My mother said, I never should
Play with the gypsies in the wood.
If I did, she would say
'Naughty little girl to disobey'.

What did I tell you?

I said it would end in tears.

I don't find satisfaction in being right all the
time, you know.

Domestic skills

Mothers are very supportive of efforts here, no matter how dismal. They can show great skill and diplomacy with phrases such as these which pass into family lore …

It'll be better when it's pressed.

No one will notice.

You can only see it in the light.

Perhaps you could dye it.

A scarf would help.

Do you think that colour is quite right?

Here, let me do it.

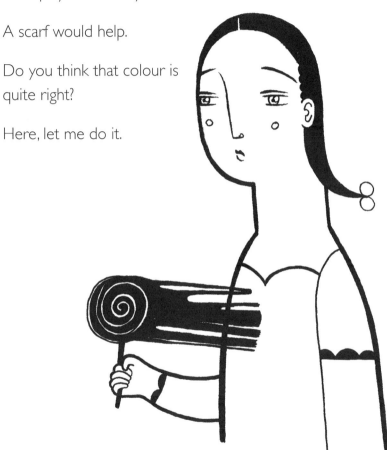

Objets trouvés

Not lost but gone before.

If it were any closer it would bite you.

If I come up there and find it,
there'll be trouble.

You'd forget your head if it wasn't screwed on.

Education

You are being educated for a
career, not a job.

Don't they teach you
anything at school
nowadays?

Two and two makes four —
at least it did when I
went to school.

Homework

Have you done your homework?

Are you sure? Fine, then you can play.

Darling, why did you wait till this
morning to tell me the project on the
great artists of the Renaissance
was due today?

Precautions 3

Take a clean hankie.

On learning by example

Don't do as I do — do as I say.

Deaf wish

Are you listening to me?

Honestly, it all goes in one ear and out the other.

It's like talking to a brick wall.

Family codes

FHB – Family Hold Back (when there isn't enough to go around)

HKLP – Holds Knife Like Pen

HFLC – Holds Fork Like Cello

PDLE – *pas devant les enfants* (not in front of the children)

Maternal tales

Who started this?

I want the truth, now …

Don't tell tales.

A slap for the tale and a slap for the teller.

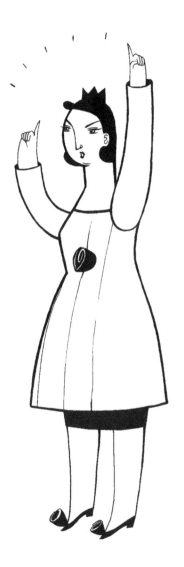

Hot and bothered

Horses sweat,
men perspire,
women merely glow.

Emergencies

I told you to go before we left
the house.

Warm words

Children don't feel the cold.

If you're cold, put a jumper on.

You'll catch your death of cold going out
dressed like that.

Are you sure you'll be warm enough?

Suitors

Do I know him?

Do I know his parents?

Why can't you bring him home — are you
ashamed of us?

What does he do for a living?

Is that a real job?

Selecting a mate

Men — neither use nor ornament.

He's not good enough for you.

You're throwing yourself away.

He'll never amount to anything.

If brains were dynamite he couldn't blow his hat off.

He couldn't lie straight in bed.

Don't say I didn't warn you.

Well, don't come crying to me.

Never trust someone who writes backwards.

Never trust someone whose eyes are too close together.

Never trust a man who wears a brown suit.

Never trust a man with a dimple in his chin.

Love

When bills come in the door, love flies out the window.

Absence makes the heart grow fonder.

There are plenty more fish in the sea.

Sex

It's just a moment's pleasure.

Boys only want one thing.

He'll never respect you in the morning.

It's the men who get the pleasure; it's the girls who get the blame.

Never do anything with a boy you'd be ashamed for me to find out.

Marriage

I married your father for better for worse, but not for lunch.

Marry a rich old man with a heart complaint.

Watch the way a man eats; can you stand to see it for the rest of your life?

You've made your bed, now you can lie in it.

Marry for money and you will spend the rest of your life earning it.

Marry in haste, repent at leisure.

What's yours is mine and what's mine's my own.

Emergency measures

Turn it inside out.

Don't take the jacket off.

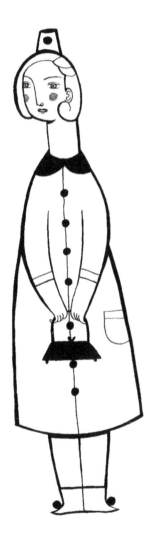

Family planning

Never fill up a house with
boys trying for a girl,
or vice versa.

On being taken for granted

This isn't a hotel, you know.

What did your last servant die of?

I won't always be here to do this for you, you know.

It's time you stood on your own two feet.

You'll be the death of me.

Household fairies

Have you tried looking in the wardrobe? The laundry fairy may have ironed it and hung it up.

No, I don't know what's for dinner. The cooking fairy has been at work all day.

Gratitude

How sharper than a serpent's tooth it is
To have a thankless child.

William Shakespeare, *King Lear*

After all I've done for you.

You'll thank me for this one day.

Mothers v. daughters

Don't you give me that look, I invented it.

What's the matter, cat got your tongue?

She is the cat's mother.

Do you think I was born yesterday?

They're not wrinkles, they're laughter lines.

Don't take that tone of voice with *me*, young lady.

If I'd spoken to *my* mother like that …

In *my* day we didn't answer back.

When I was your age …

I'm not as green as I am cabbage looking.

Pardon me for living!

When I want your opinion, I'll ask for it.

Well, if you're going to take that attitude, there's no point in discussing it.

I was young myself once you know, when dinosaurs roamed the earth.

There's no need to swear.

Sarcasm is the lowest form of wit.

When *you're* the Mummy you can have children of your own to be horrible to, but for the moment, it's my turn.

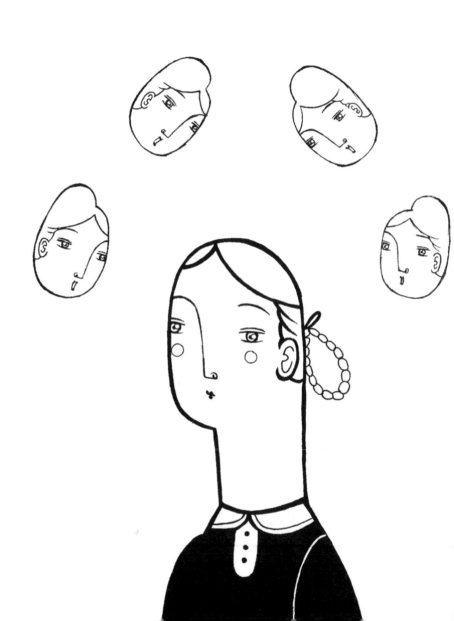

Repeating oneself

I've told you once so I won't tell you again.

If I've told you once I've told you a hundred times.

Mysteries

Who did that? Mr Nobody?

Where did you last see it?

Can't you think of anyone
but yourself?

Making faces

The wind will change and
you'll stay like that.

Precautions 4

Always carry enough money in your purse
for a phone call or a taxi home.

Arbitration

I don't care who started it — I'm finishing it!

It takes two to start a quarrel, and both are wrong.

Never let the sun go down on an argument.

Share and share alike.

Two wrongs don't make a right.

There'll be new rules in this house.

While you're under my roof you'll go by my rules.

How would you feel if someone did that to you?

Ways of saying no

Maybe …

We'll see …

Ask your father.

Retribution

God hears everything.

As ye sow so shall ye reap.

Wait till I get you home.

Wait till your father gets home.

I'll give you something to cry about in
a minute.

Once is funny, twice is not, three times
deserves a slap.

You'll be laughing on the other side of your face when I've finished with you.

Maternal flagellation

Where did I go wrong?

I've been too soft with you, that's been the problem.

I'm just a fool to myself.

Economics

Do you think I'm made of money?

Do you think money grows on trees?

Save the wrapping paper.

Keep the string.

Champagne taste and beer income.

No you can't ...

You're too young.

When you're older.

Not at your age.

You'll be grown up
soon enough.

Stay a child as long as
you can.

Don't wish your life away.

You're not a baby any more, you know.

Grow up — you're not a child.

Maternal support

You'll feel better after a nice cup of tea.

Nobody will love you like your mother.

You're better off without him.

He's not the only pebble on the beach.

Always look on the bright side

Misery loves company.

It'll seem better in the morning.

It's always darkest before the dawn.

Try and find some good in all this.

This will make you a better person.

I won't say I told you so.

Never mind, have a good cry.

Silence is golden

Least said, soonest mended.

Some things are better left unsaid.

Keep your thoughts to yourself.

Better to keep your mouth shut and have everyone think you a fool, rather than open your mouth and confirm it.

Speak up, don't mumble!

Shush, do you want everyone to hear?

There's no reason to shout, I'm not deaf!

est-
dress f my
ght with Andrew
I have seen a bea
utiful dress in th
e window of a bou
tique in tow

Confession is good for the soul

Mothers — they get you coming, they get you going. Why do they always have to know everything?

A penny for your thoughts.

If you can't tell *me*, who can you tell?

Spit it out!

On not quite telling the truth

Oh what a tangled web we weave, when first we practise to deceive!

Sir Walter Scott, *Marmion*

If you lie, you'll get a pimple on your tongue.

Precautions 5

Take a cardigan.

On gossip

While they're talking about you, they're leaving some other poor fool alone.

At least they're talking about you.

A lady only appears in the newspaper three times — birth, marriage and death. Anything else is vulgar.

Eavesdroppers never hear any good of themselves.

A secret's only a secret when you don't tell anyone.

If you can't say something nice about someone, don't say anything at all.

Sanctuary

No, I haven't been in your room.

I just went in to clean it.

I haven't been through your
personal things.

No, I would never read your
diary, darling, I didn't even know
you kept one.

The wardrobe is for clothes not the floor.

How can you live like this?

At *least* make your bed.

Home is where the heart is

A child enters your home and makes so much noise for 20 years that you can hardly stand it: then departs, leaving the house so silent that you think you will go mad.

John Andrew Holmes

I'm changing the locks when you're 18.

Hello, stranger.

So, couldn't you have telephoned?

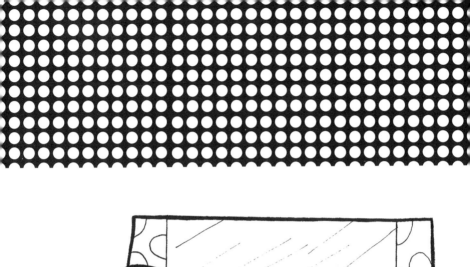

Yes, my darling daughter

Mother may I go and bathe?
Yes, my darling daughter.
Hang your clothes on yonder tree,
but don't go near the water.

You can go to the party but I want you home by ten.

The price of motherhood is eternal vigilance

Where have you been till this time of night?

I know what you've been doing.

Have you been with a boy?

What's that on your neck?

I can't sleep till I know you're home.

I heard you come in at 2.00 a.m.

You can't lie to me, I'm your mother.

I've got eyes in the back of my head, you know.

The demon drink

Never drink on an empty head.

That's not a lady's drink.

Gin makes you depressed, whisky makes you drunk and vodka makes you everybody's.

Never leave your drink unattended — a man can slip something into it and take advantage of you.

I'm bored ...

If you're bored, you're boring.

Yes, my darling son

No one will ever be good enough for you.

Leave it alone, it's not a toy.

You're just like your father.

You don't get that from *my*
side of the family.

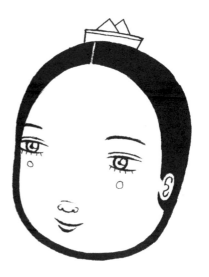

Mother's Day

It's children's day every day — today's *my* day.

It's lovely darling. What *is it*, exactly?

I'll use it every day.

Is a simple cup of tea in bed too much to ask?

Precautions 6

When in doubt — don't.

Memories

You were such a beautiful baby,
I don't know what happened.

Eternity

A son is a son till he gets him a wife, but a daughter's a daughter all her life.

The last word

God could not be everywhere,
therefore he created mothers.

Jewish proverb